GW00630990

A Touch of Christmas

A Touch of Christmas

Easy to make Stockings and Gifts

Pamela Allardice

Illustrated by Kate Mitchell

Angus&Robertson
An imprint of HarperCollins*Publishers*

Contents

Home-made Sweets and Biscuits 19

Christmas Stockings 41

Introduction

"Christmas won't be Christmas without any presents," grumbled Jo in Louisa May Alcott's classic, *Little Women*. Jo and her sisters did not, you will remember, receive many gifts that year, but they did learn that giving presents was just as much fun. They spent all their pocket money on their beloved "Marmee", buying her slippers, cologne, gloves and some handkerchiefs.

During the ancient Roman holiday of Saturnalia, it is recorded that children exchanged candles and plants. However, it is a relatively recent custom to give children toys as gifts at Christmas. Before 1850, store-bought presents were only for the privileged. Then, during the second half of the nineteenth century, toys such as jigsaw puzzles, whistles, beautifully illustrated children's books and board games became widely available. In Victorian times, people were particularly fond of exchanging such gifts among family, and also giving gifts to those less fortunate than themselves. Christmas charity boxes, containing presents of food and money were distributed to the "deserving poor" of the parish, usually on Boxing Day. During hard times, such as the worldwide Depression of the 1930s, local charity groups substituted new boots and clothing for toys.

Home-made gifts and toys have long held a special place in our affections. And, despite the wonderful array of brightly coloured plastic toys now available, most children will still love a handmade soft toy like a rag doll. Then, as now, these pretty and practical gifts can easily be made at home and will be just as welcome as store-bought ones. Modern hype can turn present-giving into quite a complicated and worrisome task. It is best to remember that Christmas presents for children are the most important ones and that often it is the simplest things which give the most pleasure. It is also worth remembering the few lines which begin: "For God so loved the world that he gave ..." Here we have the true spirit of Christmas giving which should characterise the festive season.

HOME-MADE
Gifts

Scented Pin Cushion

Make sewing even more enjoyable by slipping a spicy sachet inside a pincushion you are making. Combine equal amounts of rose geranium leaves and rosemary needles; add a few crushed cloves, slivers of nutmeg and a pounded cinnamon stick for an aromatic treat. Every time the recipient presses a needle or pin home, a puff of scent will be released, perfuming both the work and the seamstress.

Fragrant Drawer Liners

These are made by stitching fine organdy or taffeta rectangular pouches to fit the base of drawers. Stitch on three sides, fill loosely with a fragrant potpourri mixture, then stitch the fourth seam. Placed in each drawer, these padded liners will effectively perfume clothes, as well as the room, for many months.

LAVENDER "BOTTLE" OR WAND

A favourite gift for young and old is the scented "bottle" or wand. Collect together about 30 lavender flowers on stalks as long as possible, with a narrow ribbon about 1 metre (3 feet) long. Tie together tightly, just below the flowers. Bend the stems back gently below the ribbon so they form a "cage" over the flowers, and tie the bottom of the stems together. Weave the long end of ribbon over and under the stems, moving down the wand till all the lavender is enclosed. Stitch the ribbon ends securely and finish with a bow.

Perfumed Oven Mitts

These are very easy to make. Simply unpick a seam and tuck dried lavender or a brisk-smelling herb, such as rosemary, into the padding where the palm will go. Then sew it up. A refreshing burst of fragrance will be released each time the mitt is squeezed around a hot dish.

Sweet Sleep Pillow

His Majesty George III was said to rely upon a specially scented pillow to "... relieve him from that protracted wakefulness under which he laboured for so long a time." To make a restful pillow for sleep, stitch two pieces of muslin approximately 30 cm (12 in) square together on three sides. The dried mixture of scented herbs and leaves may be mixed directly with the pillow stuffing or put into cotton sachet bags and placed inside the pillow. The scented pillow may then be slipped into a decorative pillow case made from a dainty fabric and decorated with embroidery, appliqué or lace. Try the following combination for truly sweet dreams:

25 g (1 oz) lavender flowers
25 g (1 oz) bergamot
15 g (½ oz) rose geranium leaves
15 g (½ oz) lemon verbena
15 g (½ oz) jasmine petals
1 cinnamon stick, pounded
1 tablespoon orris root powder

Scrapbook

Most children love to have somewhere to house their many different collections — postcards, labels, phone cards, recipes, greeting cards, and pressed flowers, for example. Use two pieces of heavy cardboard for the cover, scoring 4 cm (1 ½ in) from one long side of each so the book will open easily. Bend cardboard pieces back on scored lines and cover outside of both smoothly with adhesive paper.

Make an appropriate design for the cover — initials can be pasted or painted on, for example. Cut pieces of firm art paper 1.25 cm (½ in) smaller than covers on three sides only (when scrapbook is assembled, the sides of the pages with the holes in should be flush with the spine). Use a paper punch to make holes in the paper, then punch holes along scored side of each cover to match. Thread all the pieces together, using ribbon, leather thonging or bright raffia or string. Don't forget to start the scrapbook off by pasting in a few samples. Or, if the collection is likely to be swapped, slip in a pack of adhesive photograph "corners" or stamp protectors, available from newsagents, so the cards or labels can be moved around without damage.

Lucky Clover Bookmark

Four-leaf clovers are supposed to bring good luck. If you look long and hard you may be able to locate one. However, for this craft, the more common three-leaf variety will do very well indeed. You will need:

clover, preferably four-leaf, but any kind will do

plain white paper

heavy book

stiff art or construction paper, in colour of your choice

liquid white glue

paintbrush

tweezers

Place the clover between two sheets of plain white paper and press between pages of a heavy book for three to four days. Check to see that it has dried thoroughly and, if it has, gently take it out and set it aside. Cut a strip of the coloured art paper 17 x 3.5 cm (7 x 1½ in). Use the paintbrush to paint the back of the dried clover carefully with the glue, then pick it up with the tweezers and place it on one end of the paper strip. Set aside and allow to dry thoroughly before use.

Can Stilts

A pair of can stilts are quick and easy to make and provide plenty of fun for younger children. You will need:

2 large cans (steel, not aluminium)
2 pieces of thick string 1.5 metres (4 feet) long
acrylic paint
hammer and nail, or awl

Select cans which are the same height and of a width that a child can comfortably stand upon. Wash the cans and remove any labels, then decorate with acrylic paint — numbers, zig-zags or the child's initials are all good ideas. When the paint is dry, make two holes opposite each other at the closed end of the cans, using either the awl or the hammer and nail. Finish holes' edges with a metal file to ensure they will not fray the strings.

Thread a piece of string through each can and join the two ends with the reef knot. This means the strings can be adjusted to suit each user by shifting the knot.

Rag Doll

Little children love old-fashioned rag dolls. Either purchase a pattern from your haberdashery shop, or draft a simple body shape onto plain white cotton or lawn and cut out two pieces. Remember to leave a seam allowance all the way around. Put right sides together and stitch around, leaving a gap in the side. Turn right side out and stuff doll with kapok or soft fibre wadding, both available from craft shops. A nice touch is to add a few dried scented flowers, such as lavender, before sewing up the toy.

Embroider a face and stitch on hair made of lengths of coloured embroidery silk or fine wool. A wardrobe is now in order — a pinny, bonnet and skirt or waistcoat and shorts are all very simple to make and may be decorated with lace trim, bows or small buttons.

Treasure Box

An inexpensive and very special gift is to decorate an ordinary strongbox — preferably one with a lock and key. Paint the box with silver, pastel or bright gloss paint, then decorate with hearts, ribbons, shells, pebbles, lengths of coloured wool or sequins.

Padded Coat-hanger

Fill a muslin bag the length of a wooden coat-hanger — approximately 30 x 9 cm (12 x 4 in) — with a delicately scented potpourri mix. Then glue it into place on top of the hanger, adding a few stitches around the hanger's central wire hook to secure, and wrap strips of thin foam sheeting around both, tying firmly with cotton thread. Cover with pretty silk, organza or muslin. For a finishing touch, swing a tiny bag of lace-trimmed matching fabric, embroidered with the recipient's initials, from the hook.

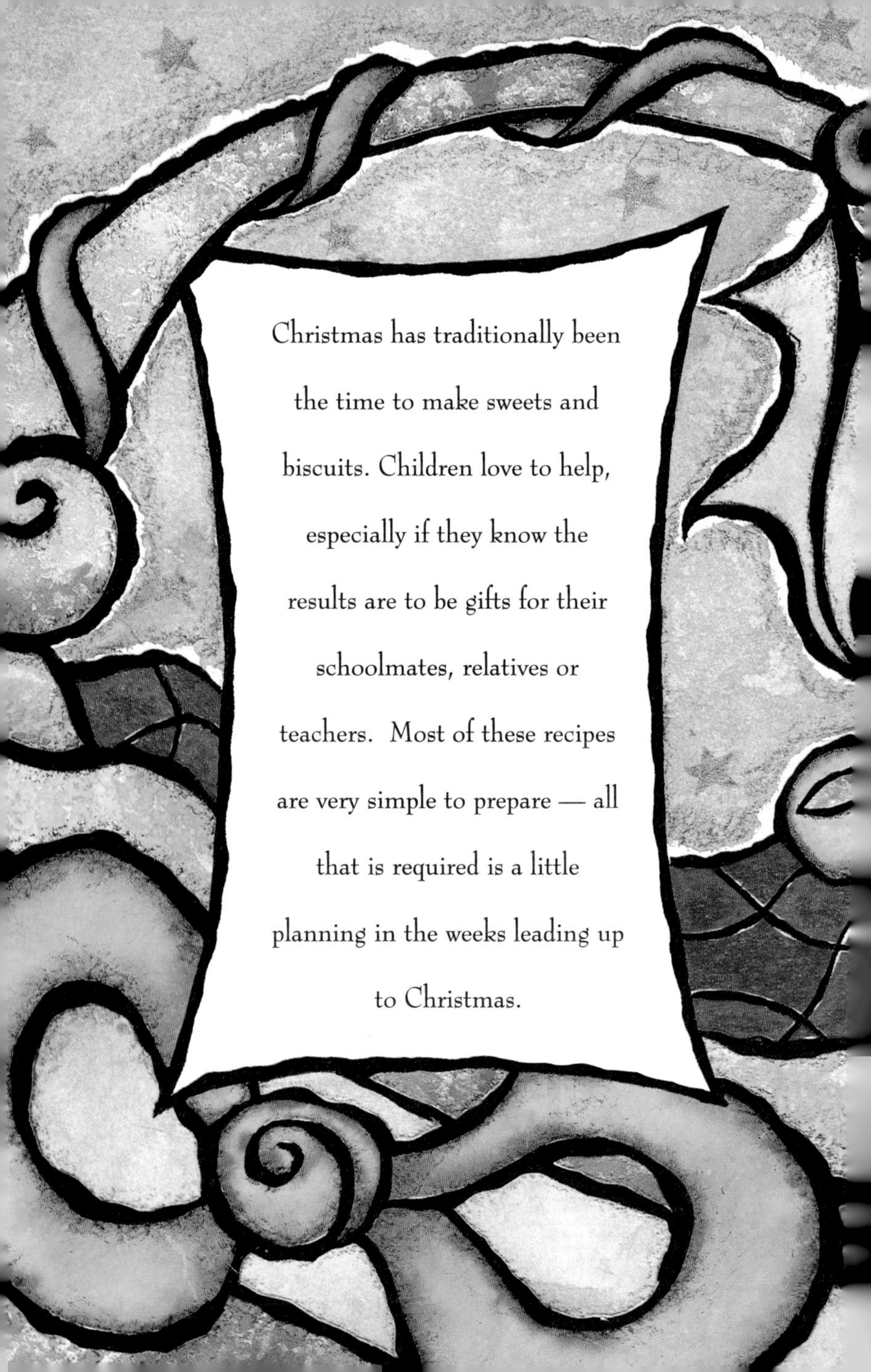

Christmas has traditionally been the time to make sweets and biscuits. Children love to help, especially if they know the results are to be gifts for their schoolmates, relatives or teachers. Most of these recipes are very simple to prepare — all that is required is a little planning in the weeks leading up to Christmas.

HOME-MADE SWEETS
& Biscuits

Scottish Shortbread

250 g (8 oz) butter
180 g (6 oz) caster sugar
zest of 1 lemon, grated
1 egg, beaten
500 g (1 lb) plain flour, sifted
pinch salt
crystallised or candied citrus peel, optional

Preheat oven to 180°C (350°F) and butter a baking sheet. Cream butter and sugar, add lemon zest and beat well. Add beaten egg, then sifted flour, and salt. Roll out to about 1.25 cm (½ in) thickness and cut into circles or squares, marking the tops with a decorative pattern (traditionally, the tines of a fork are used). Garnish with crystallised or candied peel, if desired, and place on buttered baking sheet. Bake for 20 to 30 minutes. Cool for 10 minutes then turn onto rack.

Nougat Tartlets

Pastry

75 g (2 ½ oz) butter
180 g (6 oz) self raising flour, sifted
pinch salt
cold water

Filling

1 tablespoon apricot jam
1 egg white
50 g (2 oz) sugar
50 g (2 oz) desiccated coconut
25 g (1 oz) ground almonds
30 g (1 oz) chopped almonds
1 lemon
1 teaspoon vanilla essence
1 teaspoon brown sugar

Preheat oven to 200°C (400°F) and lightly butter a patty pan tray.

Tartlet cases: Rub butter into sifted flour and salt, working to a firm dough by adding a little water at a time. Knead until smooth. Roll out dough on a well floured board to 0.3 cm (⅛ in) thickness and, using tartlet cutter, cut circular shapes. Use these to line the patty pans. Spread pastry with thin layer of jam.

Nougat filling: Beat egg white till firm, then add sugar, coconut, ground almonds, and chopped almonds. Add juice and grated zest of lemon, and vanilla essence. Spoon into tartlet cases, then sprinkle with brown sugar. Bake for 12 to 15 minutes, or until mixture has set. Let cool on racks, then dust with icing sugar, if desired.

Chocolate Macaroons

250 g (8 oz) ground almonds
125 g (4 oz) finely grated dark chocolate
250 g (8 oz) caster sugar
4 egg whites, stiffly beaten

Preheat oven to 180°C (350°F) and butter a baking sheet. Combine almonds, chocolate, and sugar in bowl. Add beaten egg whites and work mixture to a firm paste. Place teaspoonfuls of mixture on baking sheet, and bake slowly for approximately 20 minutes till firm.

Jewel Biscuits

6 tablespoons butter
250 g (8 oz) sugar
2 eggs
375 g (12 oz) plain flour
2 teaspoons baking powder
315 g (10 oz) thick raspberry jam
extra sugar, for dipping

Preheat oven to 200°C (400°F). Cream butter and sugar. Add eggs, then flour and baking powder, mixing well to form firm dough. Using your hands, roll dough into small balls, dip into sugar and press sugar into outside of dough. Flatten biscuits slightly and make a dent in the top of each; fill with raspberry jam. Bake for approximately 20 minutes till firm.

Candied Citrus Peel

2 lemons

3 oranges

1 lime

1 teaspoon salt

700 g (1 ½ lb) sugar

water

icing sugar

Halve fruit, place in large bowl or crock, mix with salt and enough water to cover; leave for 3 days. Lift out and leave to drain on a rack for a further 24 hours. Scoop pulp from fruit shells and slice peel thinly. Make a syrup by combining sugar with sufficient water to cover, then cook mixture in a non-aluminium saucepan till boiling. Place peel in boiling syrup and cook for 20 minutes, then drain rinds for 24 hours, reserving syrup. Reboil syrup and add rinds again. Cook for a further

20 minutes, then allow rinds to cool in the syrup. Drain rinds, sprinkle with icing sugar and dry them off thoroughly by placing in slow oven for approximately 40 minutes, or longer, till quite dry. Store in a dry place in airtight containers. Candied peel will keep for 3 to 4 weeks, though it will spoil if exposed to moisture.

Turkish Delight

icing sugar, sifted
1 kg (2 lb) white sugar
water
juice of 1 lemon
2 egg whites
110 g (4 oz) cornflour
extra water
rosewater
extra icing sugar

Grease two 25 x 15 cm (10 x 5½ in) slice pans with butter; dust one liberally with icing sugar. Combine sugar with enough water over a low heat in a non-aluminium saucepan until just boiling so as to achieve a syrupy consistency. Add lemon juice and egg whites and continue to cook, bringing gradually to the boil. In a separate bowl, dissolve cornflour in a little extra cold water. Add this to boiling sugar and egg white mixture. Cook until mixture thickens and then flavour with rosewater. Pour mixture into plain buttered tray and allow to cool slightly for approximately 10 minutes. Then, when it is firm enough, flip mixture over into sugared tray and sprinkle extra icing sugar on top. Once Delight has soaked up sugar and cooled, cut into squares and put away, dusting cut corners with extra icing sugar so squares will not stick together.

Coconut Ice

500 g (1 lb) icing sugar, sifted
pinch cream of tartar
2 egg whites
3 tablespoons condensed milk
125 g (4 oz) desiccated coconut
cochineal

Mix half the icing sugar with cream of tartar. Lightly whisk 1 egg white and add to mixture, then stir through condensed milk, mixing till smooth. Gradually add the rest of the icing sugar and the coconut, till mixture is thick. Divide mixture in half and colour one half with a few drops of cochineal. Lightly whisk the second egg white. Dust a board and rolling pin with icing sugar and roll out white half of mixture to about 1.25 cm (½ in) thickness. Brush the top with whisked egg white, then press pink layer evenly on top. Cut coconut ice into fingers or squares and leave in a dry place to harden. Store in airtight container.

Butternut Toffee

500 g (1 lb) sugar
½ cup (4 fl oz) water
1 ¼ cups (9 fl oz) light corn syrup
250 g (8 oz) butter
250 g (8 oz) finely chopped, lightly toasted hazelnuts
125 g (4 oz) bittersweet or semi-sweet cooking chocolate
coarsely chopped hazelnut halves, lightly toasted

Butter two tiny tartlet tins. Combine sugar, water, corn syrup and butter in a large non-aluminium saucepan over low heat until sugar has dissolved. Bring to boiling point and cook, stirring occasionally, till mixture reaches hard-crack stage (when a pinch of the mixture dropped into a glass of cold water will snap or crack). Remove from heat and quickly stir in finely chopped hazelnuts and coarsely chopped chocolate. Pour into prepared tins. Top each with a toasted hazelnut half and allow to cool. Store in an airtight container. Toffee will keep for up to two weeks.

Candied Almonds

250 g (8 oz) caster sugar
2 tablespoons treacle
1 tablespoon molasses
90 g (3 oz) butter
⅓ cup (4 fl oz) liquid glucose
⅔ cup (8 fl oz) condensed milk
125 g (4 oz) almonds, unblanched

Lightly oil a baking sheet and set aside. Combine sugar, treacle, molasses, butter, glucose and condensed milk in heavy-based saucepan over low heat and stir until sugar starts to melt. Continue to cook and bring to boiling point, stirring frequently with a wooden spoon until mixture is a golden, caramel colour. Dip bottom of pan in cold water to reduce heat and mix in almonds; set aside till just warm. Take small spoonfuls of almond mixture and mould into rounds on baking sheet. Chill in refrigerator till firm, then transfer to airtight container, separating layers with greaseproof paper. Candied almonds will keep for up to two weeks. Serve slightly chilled.

Rum Balls

180 g (6 oz) hazelnuts, roughly ground
125 g (4 oz) chocolate wafer biscuit crumbs
180 g (6 oz) soft brown sugar
1 ½ tablespoons light treacle
¼ cup (2 fl oz) dark rum
cocoa powder for dusting
icing sugar or coconut

Grind together nuts and biscuit crumbs in a food processor. In large bowl, work nut mixture thoroughly into sugar, treacle and rum to form firm paste. Add extra rum or biscuit crumbs until you have a texture that can be rolled into firm, bite-sized balls. Dust with cocoa, then roll alternate balls in icing sugar and coconut. Store in airtight container in cool place. These also freeze well.

Fruit and Nut Balls

225 g (8 oz) wholemeal self-raising flour
1 tablespoon sugar
pinch salt
110 g (4 oz) butter
water
1 tablespoon chopped dried figs
1 tablespoon chopped raisins
1 tablespoon chopped crystallised ginger
1 tablespoon finely chopped walnuts or pecans
½ tablespoon chopped candied peel
1 tablespoon golden syrup
1 teaspoon whisky
dash orange juice
icing sugar, for rolling

Sift flour, sugar and salt together, then rub butter into flour mixture. Add enough water to make a stiff dough, then mix in figs, raisins, ginger, nuts, peel, golden syrup, whisky and orange juice. With your hands, roll fruit and nut mixture, a quarter of a teaspoonful at a time, into balls. Bake in a 220°C (425°F) oven for 10 to 12 minutes. Allow to cool on racks, then roll in icing sugar while still warm. Store between layers of greaseproof paper in an airtight lidded container for up to 3 weeks before use.

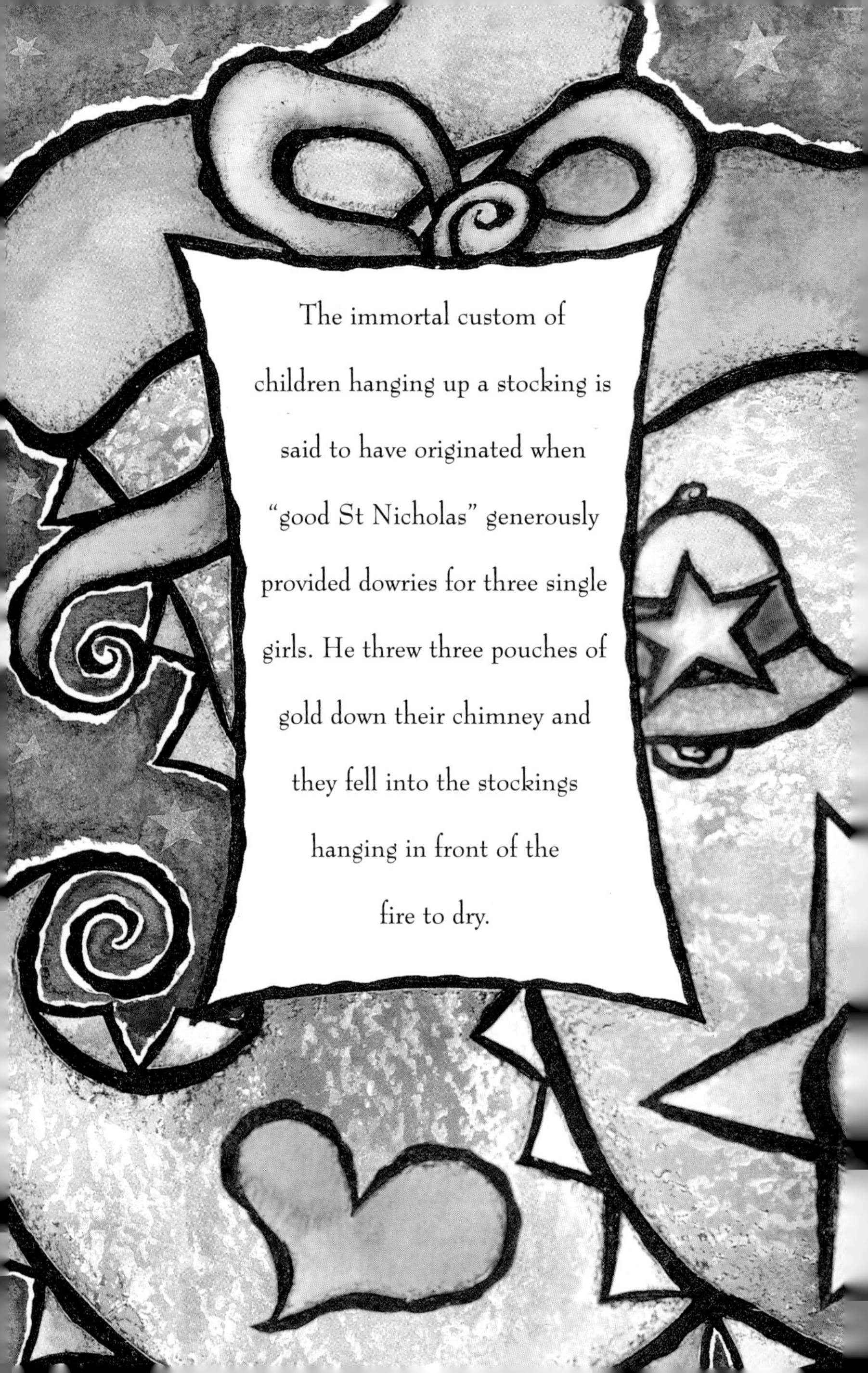

The immortal custom of children hanging up a stocking is said to have originated when "good St Nicholas" generously provided dowries for three single girls. He threw three pouches of gold down their chimney and they fell into the stockings hanging in front of the fire to dry.

CHRISTMAS
Stockings

Colourful Stocking

Felt is a terrific material for making bright, simple Christmas stockings. It is easy to sew or glue and, because the pieces do not need hemming, children can cut out all sorts of different shapes — hearts, leaves, circles and faces — to decorate their own stockings.

Get one large piece of felt. Make a paper pattern for the stocking shape and cut out two from the felt. Stitch a strip of contrasting felt to the top edges of the stocking and decorate one or both sides before sewing the two sides together. (Tip: the stocking does not really have to be turned inside out again after it is sewn; the exposed seam edge looks great if you trim it with pinking shears.) Sew or glue a loop to the top and thread a brass or plastic curtain ring through it.

Stocking Fillers

Very young children are interested in everything and will happily play with many materials other than shop-bought toys. The following are often popular in stockings:

A round rosy apple stuffed in the toe and an orange in the heel; and

A shiny new coin (traditionally, it was an English penny) is often included in a stocking to bring good fortune.

Then fill the stocking with popular playthings — crayons, a colouring-in book, a doll, a puzzle, a whistle, felt pens, striped socks, knuckle bones (jacks), dice and a ball. Any selection of homemade sweets will be welcome in a child's stocking.

Here are some other quick and easy stocking fillers you can make:

Magic Wand

Cut a length of 1 cm (¼ in) diameter dowel rod. Cut a piece of silver or gold foil, spray liberally with adhesive and wrap around rod several times. Decorate by sticking on coloured stars or glitter and make one large star out of a silver paper doily and glue to the top of the wand.

Fairy Slippers

Turn a prosaic pair of bedroom "jiffy" slippers into a very special present for a little girl by stitching a cluster of little bells on the toes. A rosette of bright pink ribbons, a fat green felt frog, sequins or silver braid may also be used to good effect.

Finger Puppets

Take an old glove (cotton or leather are better than wool) and snip off the fingers. Turn the edges under and stick or glue securely in place. Decorate "face" with tiny buttons or beads for nose and yarn for hair.

Gift Wrapping

Rustling paper and lavish ribbon bows are as much a part of Christmas as the gifts themselves. Before paper was printed by the roll, wrappings were prepared by hand and the givers would take much time and care to make their gifts attractive. Some ideas for wrapping are given below.

Using plain brown paper, apply gold or copper paint in different ways for different effects, e.g. stripes or criss-cross diagonals, a spattered look by dripping or drizzling paint, or a sponged effect by pressing a paint-dipped sponge randomly onto the paper.

Make a potato printing block: cut a potato in half and cut away a pattern, leaving a raised shape. Rinse thoroughly, blot dry, then dip in paint or dye before printing on paper. Terrific effects can be made by overprinting the same shape in different colours. Wetting the sheet of paper before applying colour will give a soft, fuzzy effect.

"Ice cream cone" wrapping is a clever way to disguise small or oddly-shaped gifts, particularly if the recipient is a curious and nimble-fingered child! Simply spread out a large sheet of paper, roll it narrowly at one end to form a cone and then tape the length securely together. Stuff base of cone with tissue paper and then insert the wrapped gift. Cover gift with sheets of cotton wool, pulling at it to make it fluffy and so it "melts" down the side of the cone. Sprinkle glitter on top of the ice cream, add a red Christmas bauble as a "cherry" and tape the gift tag to the cone.

"Glitter paper" is particularly striking when used on large flat or box-shaped gifts. Simply mark out your design or message, for instance the recipient's name, with glue, on plain wrapping paper. Then, liberally sprinkle the letters of your message with glitter. Let dry for at least half an hour so glitter does not come off easily when paper is folded.

Be imaginative — funny faces and Santa Clauses are easily made from cut-out pieces of adhesive paper; or, spread glue in a design, e.g. a wreath, a tree, a star, and sprinkle generously with shiny confetti; wrap with contrasting papers half and half, joined at the seam with coordinating ribbon; or use cut outs from last year's Christmas cards as decorations for packages.

For smaller gifts, a silk scarf or printed handkerchief could provide an appealing wrapper. Cardboard boxes, saved over the year, can be covered or lined with pretty fabric and stencilled.

Gift Tags and Containers

Tags can be made from paper or light card and cut to any shape (square, oval, or circular, for instance) which suits the design you have in mind. Cut out with pinking shears and add a shiny ribbon loop, raffia or gold braid. Add a final personal touch by decorating the tag or card with dried or pressed flowers, cut-out shapes or snippets of lace or ribbon rosettes.

Save attractive bottles, jars and crocks throughout the year, and use to display home-made chutneys and jellies. Store-bought adhesive labels can be attractively personalised with stencils, felt markers or even crayons. For very special gifts, look in antique or old wares shops for glass jars or decanters which may be filled with a favourite jam or herb vinegar.

Wicker baskets and hampers make good containers for cakes and biscuits, or selections of potted jams and vinegars. Individual sweets, such as fudge or toffee, look pretty and are easier to handle if they are placed in little paper or foil cups and then packed in layers separated by greaseproof paper.

Ribbons and Bows

Ribbons can be used in many ways. Choose a colour that enhances the paper you have selected. Try any of the following ideas for really attractive gifts.

Criss-cross — hold one end of the ribbon at one end of the box. Wind the ribbon around lengthwise, cross over at the starting point and wind around the width. Fasten at start point. Repeat.

Left-over bow — save all the short lengths of ribbon and trim them to between 10–15 cm (4–6 in) long. Tie tightly together in the middle with fuse wire, cover with a thin strip of ribbon and tease out ends.

"Poinsettia" bow — using flat, wide, crisp, red ribbon, cut out 3 sets of double petals, one 8 cm (3 in) long, one 6.5 cm (2 ½ in) long and one 5 cm (2 in) long. Arrange petals on top of one another and tie together with a thin, knotted piece of shiny yellow ribbon. Separate all the petals by tying back and forth across the flower in all directions with the ends of the yellow ribbon.

An Angus & Robertson Publication

Angus&Robertson, an imprint of
HarperCollins*Publishers*
25 Ryde Road, Pymble, Sydney NSW 2073, Australia
31 View Road, Glenfield, Auckland 10, New Zealand
77–85 Fulham Palace Road, London W6 8JB, United Kingdom
10 East 53rd Street, New York NY 10022, USA

First published in Australia in 1994

National Library of Australia
Cataloguing-in-Publication data:

Allardice, Pamela, 1958-.
A touch of Christmas: easy to make stockings and gifts.
ISBN 0 207 18409 7.
Christmas cookery. 2. Handicraft. I. Title. II. Title: Easy to make stockings and gifts.

641.566

Designed by Robyn Latimer

Printed in Australia by Griffin Press, Adelaide

9 8 7 6 5 4 3 2 1
97 96 95 94